REFLECTIONS

A book of mystic roman... y.

BRIGITTA D'ARCY

*To Jane 14/02/03
with love
Brigitta D'Arcy*

PHANTOM PRESS

OLNEY BUCKINGHAMSHIRE

REFLECTIONS OF THE HEART

A book of mystic romantic and evocative poetry.

Copyright © Brigitta D'Arcy 2001

All Rights Reserved

No part of this book may be reproduced in any form by photocopying or by any electronic or mechanical means, including information storage or retrieval systems, without permission in writing from the copyright owner and the publisher of this book.

ISBN

This first edition published 2001 by
PHANTOM PRESS
OLNEY BUCKINGHAMSHIRE

Printed in Great Britain by
Tollwood, 18 Royal Gardens, Rowlands Castle, Hampshire

Also by Brigitta D'Arcy

LE FANTOME

A continuation of Gaston Leroux's
The Phantom of the Opera.

Acknowledgements

I would like to thank all my friends, without whose help and encouragement it would have been difficult to produce this book.

Jim and Linda Williams, Margaret Nicholas, Jane of Words Bookshop, Sylvia, Michael and Russell.

A special thank you to David, Rupert and Roland. Without Their help and expertise there would have been no CD

Also a special thank you to my daughter Janet for her illustrations and the design for the front cover.

REFLECTIONS OF THE HEART

A book of mystic romantic and evocative poetry.

Poetry in this book is also available on CD.
Brought magically to life by the captivating voice of actor David Kerby-Kendall and the ethereal delicate harp music composed and performed by Rupert Parker. It is a perfect oasis of peace and tranquillity in a turbulent and stressful world.

CD Produced and directed by Roland Harris.

REFLECTIONS OF THE HEART

A book of mystic romantic and evocative poetry

Illustrations and cover design by Janet Hays

FOR DAVID

Echoes of a forgotten life

Ghosts of the past
        float through my dreams
trailing echoes of forgotten life.

Fleeting image of a love that was
        haunting my immortal soul.
binding my heart
        with unbreakable bonds.

A face in the shadows
        a face I once knew
that yet eludes my eyes.

A lyrical alluring voice
        beseeching, compelling
whispers in my mind
        remember me, remember me.

I know I have been here before
        my heart was ensnared
infinite eons ago by that
        enchanting mystic voice.

Now my soul is searching
        grieving, yearning
for the love that was.

Oh return, return to me
        come out of the shadows
advance into radiant luminous light
        and let the fiery flame of love
consume us in its burnished glow.

Love Light

Two beings, tall and slender
        stretch out their arms
to one another.

But wait, love's expression
        in the dimension of the form
follows a thought.

For thought is the soul
        and the soul is the core.
The soul is unique
        it's the souls that speak...

Speak to one another
        longing to share
an abundance of love
        in the presence of the light.

For the light is love
        and love is the light
that illuminates the soul
        and enriches the heart.

So love one another
        with your souls
let in the light
        and radiate.

Immortal Beloved

My immortal beloved
        only in my dreams
you come to me
        from your other dimension.

We met and we loved
        in another lifetime.
Our souls were bonded
        a long time ago.

I was reborn to
        this physical form
but you stayed behind
        in your heavenly home.

Thus torn asunder
        we weep and we wail
our bond of souls
        is forever, eternal.

Oh, Immortal beloved
        fold me in your arms
and hold me close.
        Keep me safely near you.

Then we dance, we rejoice
        exult and embrace.
Our souls are one again
        in the darkness of night.

For a Friend

Angels and moonbeams
        sun and stars
dreams caught in a rainbow
        float gently down
around you.

Like gossamer whisps
        they encircle you
they caress you.

They are summoned
        to lighten your future
and bring joy
        in life's varied path.

Aspects

All the facets
        of a crystal
Mirror the facets
        of heart and soul.

The beautiful rainbows
        sparkling in the crystal
mirror the facets
        of love and light.

All the facets
        together are needed
to make a whole.
        Without darkness
there is no light.

Elusive Lover

My hollow footsteps
        echo on the icy cobbles
of this silent town.

Houses loom darkly
        in the misty gloom
undulating shadows
        stretch and weave
long tendrils of sorrow.

No breeze stirs
        no sound is heard
but the painful howl
        of my heart.

I crawled into the
        deepest corner of my soul
hoping there to find
        warmth and solace.

But all I see is your face
        all I hear is your voice
there is no solace, no warmth
        without the glow of your love.

You came into my life
        like a flaming comet
then stole your way into my heart.

But when I tried to hold you
            you dissolved into nothing
leaving me holding
            only armfuls of shadows
and broken dreams.

My hollow footsteps
            in this cold and silent town
echo but my pain and grief.

Soul Bond

All my life I waited for you
          I painted your picture
in my mind.

I found you, alas too late.
          You are still mortal
of this earth.

Forever my spirit
          will yearn for you.
Rising into the night
          to find you.
To hold you here
          in my heavenly realm.

Through the mists of time
          I see your lovely face,
behind pink tinted clouds
          that separate our worlds.

But one moon drenched night
          the veils will part.
Then will I wait
          to take your hand.

Together our joyous souls
          bonded in eternal love
will spiral, will fly
          to dwell in heavenly light.

Quest for the Soulmate

Darkness sweeps in
        across the tranquil sky
and one by one the stars embroider
        the canvas of the night.

Mysterious and graceful
        the golden moon shines
behind dark silhouettes of trees.

Once more my soul is searching
        for your spirit my beloved.
Oh would that my soul
        free of earthly ballast
could stay with you forever.

Centuries of longing
        and centuries of pain
metamorphose in the
        secret of the night.

Oh my spirit lover
        open wide your heart
and hide me in
        your swirling cloak.

Take my hand and lead me
        up some golden stairway
and let me drown again
        in the deep pools
of your dark eyes.

Then two souls who belong
        will unite in ecstacy
and explode in a symphony of joy.

A symphony of music of the night
        composed by angels who
guard the spirits of the light.

Written words

The words have been written
        too late to recall.
They tell of my love
        for a beautiful soul.

They tell of the years
        of all my waiting
the years of lonely longing
        for the soulmate
of my dreams.

They tell of the long search
        through life after life
for the one true love
        each one of us is given.

The words have been written
        They cannot be recalled
revealing my love
        and the secret of my heart.

Yes I have found him
        as yet he is unaware.
But should he read
        these written words
my love will stand before him
        unmasked, exposed, unveiled.

Count Dracula's Search

In the land
           Beyond the forest
Count Dracula strides
           the night.
Pale moon gleaming
           on his pallid face.

Softly he calls the
           children of the night.
They lift their heads
           and howl their answer.

On silent pads
           they come and join him.
They understand his needs.

Night after night
           his thirst drives him
in his lonely hunt.

Nobel born to
           the house of Dracul.
Brave warrior of ages past
           immortal and alone.

Searching the world
           for his own true love.
He wrote her name
           with a blood dipped quill,
Elizabeta.... Elizabeta ...

Hundreds of years
>   he walked this earth
through all the
>   changing centuries.

A prince of darkness
>   in his flowing cloak.
Striding the night
>   to search for his
long lost princess.

Empty Arms

Once more I walk
        the streets of this city
alone with my anguished heart.

So many questions
        torture my restless mind
why did you leave?
        Where are you now?
Why did we have to part?

No answer comes to me.
        Only the wayward wind
sighs in the trees
        and the rain weeps with me.

All my dreams
        bear your name
you and only you can
        fulfil the deepest need
of my mind and soul.

But.... you left...
        Left me alone
With nothing but my sorrow
        To fill my empty arms.

The Silence of the Night

The silence of the night
    hovers over the sleeping earth.
Darkness enshrouds the heavens
    in soft swirling shadows.

In the silence of the night
    my secret dreams take wing
And I send you my angel
    to proclaim my love.

In the silence of the night
    my soul may speak to you
when no one else can hear
    the language of my love.

In the silence of the night
    I have known your soul
since time began
    and when I look into your eyes
I know I'm coming home.

Love and Music are forever

My dark angel
        you came to me
from the mists
        of ancient times.

Draped in black veils
        you came to me.
Remember our promise
        it was forever you sighed.

You serenaded me
        with celestial music
and showered me
        with crystal gems.

You danced with me
        and our passion flared
leaving trails of blazing fire
        across a midnight sky.

My dark prince, from the
        mists of ancient times
I have not forgotten
        our sacred promise of love.

Our bond was forever
        then we were torn apart
by forces unseen, unknown.

Wildly I searched the sky
        and cried an ocean of tears.
For an eternity
        I mourned for you.

My dark angel
           you came back to me.
Crystal choirs sing
           our celestial song.

My heart is overflowing
           my arms reach out to you
at last at last
           our promise is fulfilled.

Fold me in your dark wings
           and hold me to your heart.
At last we sing our song
           love and music are forever.

Message from the Eco Warrior

The lone Eco warrior
        stands at the edge of doom
his fair long hair
        blowing in the wind.

A rainbow coloured cape
        flowing from his shoulders
a beautiful crystal glowing
        and sparkling at his throat.

Gently his fingers plucked
        the strings of his guitar.
Then his hearts lament
        spiralled in the air.

Will you hear me people
        of this planet earth?
Will you hear my song?

Will you stop the violence?
        will you stop the strife?
will you stop the plunder?
        will you stop the greed?

Listen! Mother earth
        is weeping
her children
        have gone astray.

Animals are dying out
        plants and trees
are withering under
        clouds of poisonous fumes.

The ozone layer-there
           to protect us from the sun
is thinning, leaving us to burn.

The delicate eco system
           so cleverly planned
to care for us
           is crumbling, is vanishing
before my disbelieving eyes.

The eco warrior lifts
           his head to the sky
eyes streaming with tears
           and begs the angels to help.

Please let light flow
           into peoples souls
open their hearts
           before it is too late.

Let enlightenment and understanding
           take the place of scepticism
Let love and compassion
           take the place of hate and scorn.

Tell them they were guardians
           of this their planet earth
this beautiful garden
           created to give them joy.

The angels came and
           brought their message.
A few heard and were
           filled with light.

But many scorned
        the message and
continued to plunder.

Animals are still crying in pain
        trees are felled
and forests stripped bare.

Oh foolish people
        can you not see?
When there are no more
        animals or trees
when mother earth
        is slowly dying
can you not see
        that you will be no more?

The eco warrior lifts
        his arms in supplication
once more his pleading
        song streams forth.

Will you hear me
        people of this planet
will you hear me
        before it is too late?

Or carry on in
        the same old way
and see your future die........

Earth Treasures

A million insects
        dancing in the sun
filled with the joy
        of living on this earth.

Buttercups and daisies
        in the fresh green meadow
stretch their little faces
        to the life giving sun.

Graceful fronds of fern
        sway in the gentle breeze
beside a meandering stream
        by the old abbey wall.

Mother earth and brother sky
        how we should revere you.
How we should guard the treasures
        you so freely bestow.

The Healing Garden

Enter the sun washed garden
                in which you lose yourself
among sweet scented blossoms
                in sparkling rainbow hues.

Silvered dew drops
                clinging like strings of pearls
on velvet petals
                soft as angel wings.

Shadowed arbours
                swathed in sweet seclusion
Invite the soul to shed
                it's weary burden.

While merry crystal water sprites
                dance in exuberant ecstasy
to merge with pools
                of deep reflection.

Joyous sounds quivering
                on the gentle breeze
performed by winged musicians
                bid the soul to stand
in breathless admiration.

And in the woodlands
                Soft blue velvet
Drapes the ground
                In tender tranquil surrender.

While tall strong guardians
                Veiled in verdant green
Unfurl their slender branches
                In silent benediction.

Enter this enchanted garden
                In which you find yourself
And heal your wounded heart.

Take Time

Must rush, must dash
                to get more money
to buy this and that.
                No time to linger
no time to talk.

Stop! Cease this heedless
                headlong haste.
Are you not chasing
                meaningless shadows.

Does this really
                make you happy?
Is it really what you want?
                your immortal soul is crying
buried under futile waste.

When did you last stop
                to smell the scent of a rose
or watch a beautiful sunset?

When did you stand and gaze
                at the star studded sky
or admire a worthwhile painting.

When did you last listen
                to merry Mozart
or passionate Beethoven?

Open up to the beauty all around
                take time for quiet reflection
and give your soul
                the chance to unfold.

Smile at someone every day
        be loving and gentle
let your light pour forth.

And watch your soul
        rise on that rainbow
of full potential
        to its true home.

Glastonbury Tor

Sacred site, ancient holy ground
        here in these divine surroundings
new beginnings will take shape.

Golden moon beams
        touch the sacred Tor
silver star dust
        sparkling all around

Angels swathed in
        blue white light
descend in silent blessing.

Soon, the birth
        of human unity,
love and compassion
        will gather momentum.

From the seed sown long ago,
        then neglected and forgotten
will burst forth a wondrous bloom.

The divine message
        will be heard
all over the world.

And like the phoenix
        rising from the ashes
a new world will be born.

The Old Dog
Written by my daughter aged twelve

He lies in front of the fire
            so quiet and so still
now that he is old.

He dreams of bygone days
            when he was young
skipping and playing in the woods.

Now he just eats and sleeps
            he walks so slowly now,
or is everyone walking faster?

His aged head is turning silver grey
            the shiny black coat
is changing colour
            and his actions are so few.

Fewer and fewer they become
            until he just lies
in front of the fire
            and sleeps and sleeps and sleeps....

Janet Hays

Spirit of the Tree

Spirit of the old sycamore
                you have guarded
this secluded bower
                for endless centuries.

Today you wear your pretty gown
                of glistening winter white
embroidered with silver stars.

Your life force slumbers
                in you inner being
while the palely glowing moon
                hides your secret dreams.

Spirit of the tree
                talk to me of bygone days
when you were young and slender.

Your swaying branches
                whisper to me in the wind
and tell of your ancient wisdom.

Your branches stretch
                their longing arms
toward the pale blue sky.
                But your knotted roots
are anchored firmly on the ground.

In spring, your branches burst
                into buds of tender green
while bluebells and primrose
                worship at your feet.

In the heat of summer
                your canopy of leafy branches
offer cool havens of shade
                to the weary wanderer.

But in the autumn days
                you wear your most beautiful
gown of flaming orange
                jewelled with red and gold.

Spirit of the tree
                I stand before you
In respectful silence
                And thank you
For your ancient wisdom.

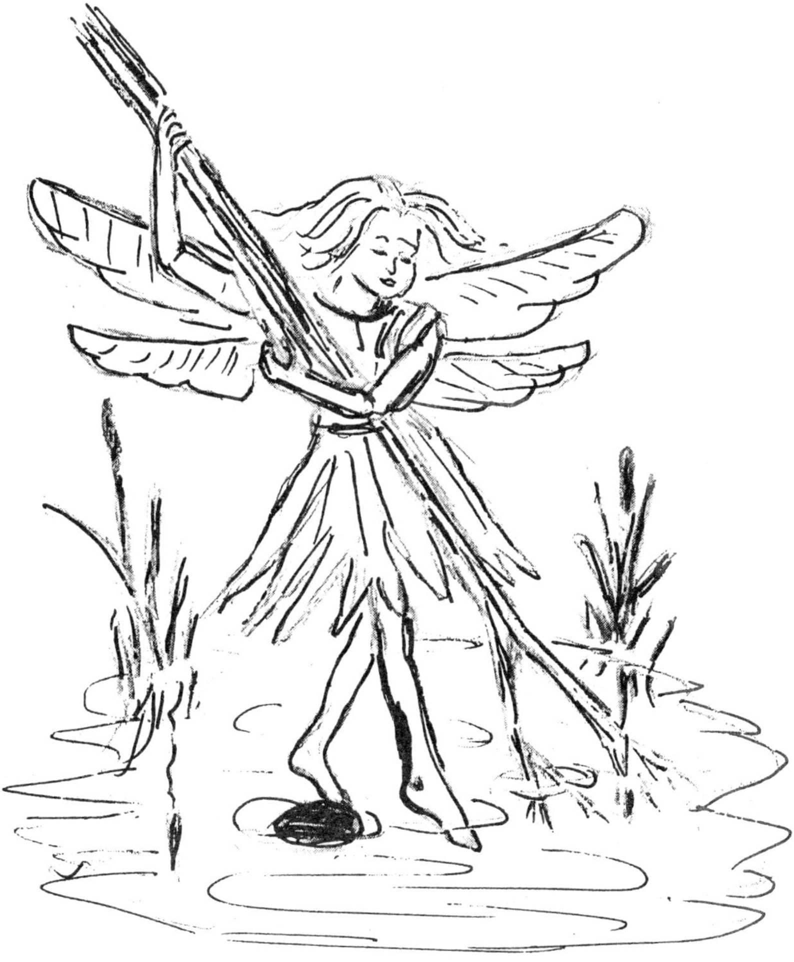

Prophesy

A vibrating white light
        hovered over the Chalice Well.
The energy sparkling,
        Whispering of things to come.

The crystalline waterfall
        beneath the holy thorn tree
grown from Arimthea's staff
        murmured gently, murmured
it has already begun.

A global awakening
        unheard of before
prophesied in all its glory
        by the emissaries light.

Fear and hate will be transmuted
        when love and compassion
take their place.

Peace will descend
        upon this planet
as the light expands
        all over this earth.

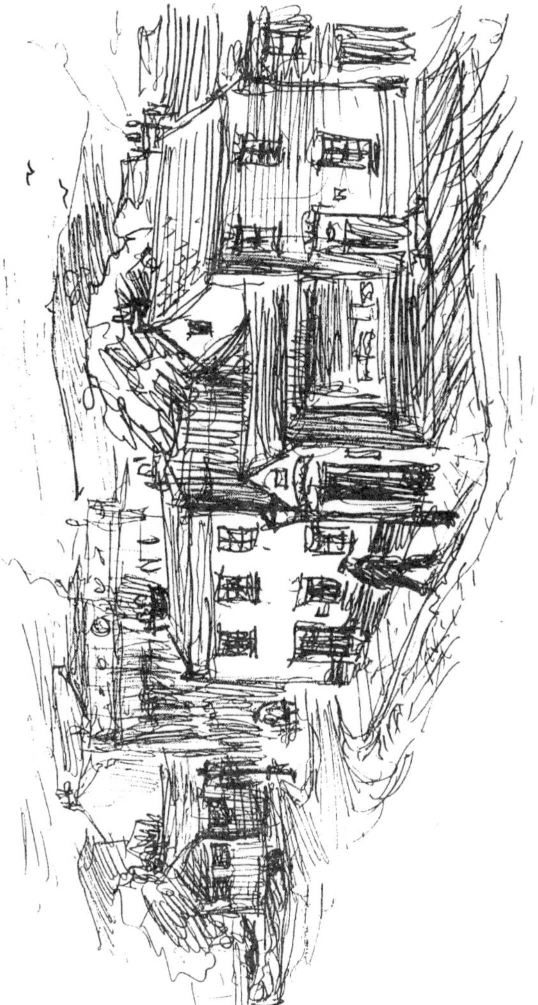

Memories

We have walked these streets before
   The houses over there look so familiar.

Over yonder stands the old school
   from whence you children
journeyed forth into life.

And over there the old corner shop
   where ham was freshly sliced
and butter patted into shape.

The old theatre's still there,
   all red plush and gilt
where we paid homage
   to music and the arts.

Do you remember the old bus station
   that used to be just there?
Gone now, never to return.

The market's still here
   and the draper on the corner.
Oh, and look, the confectioner's shop.

Out in the country, there's the farm
   and here the field, do you remember?
Where the cows surrounded you.

Further still, the moor
        strewn with gorse and heather
where we frolicked with the dogs.

Do you remember the old dam?
        where we picnicked and your
toes were frozen from the icy water.

Memories come flooding back
        of days long gone, and yet...
they seem like yesterday.

Days filled with happiness
        and laughter, some
with sadness and tears.

We have journeyed on since then
        many changes have taken place.
But one thing always remained.

The love and care we shared
        through all life's
multicoloured kaleidoscope.

The Chalice Well

Drink deep of the golden
        healing waters
at the sacred chalice well.

Find inspiration in
        the tranquil arbours
free your spirit and
        feel your soul expanding.

Fill your heart with
        love and compassion
then unite with the force
        of the universe.

Send a message
        of love and peace
bring the light of
        spiritual awakening
to all the dark
        corners of the globe.

Be a loving guardian
        of this your planet earth
then return to the sacred well
        drink from the golden chalice.

and radiate, radiate, radiate
        all the light and love
of a loving universe.

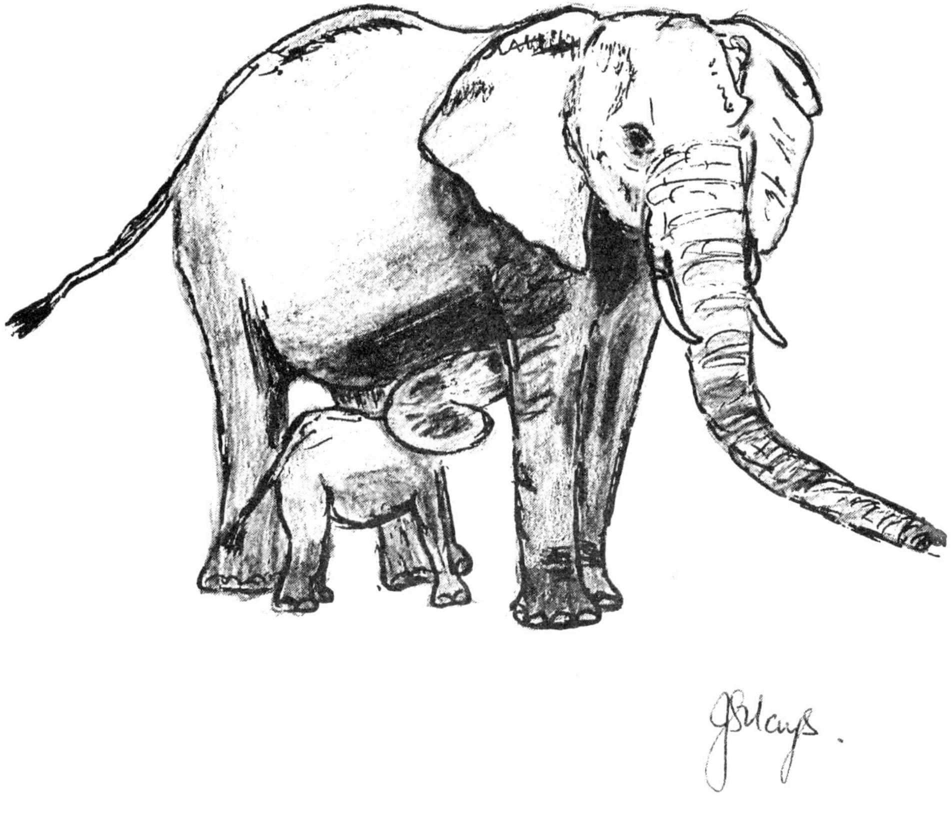

A Baby Elephant's Lament and Plea

A Baby Elephant
              stood crying
by the side
              of his dead mother.

His tiny trunk
              probing her mutilated head
so carefully, so tenderly

Then he swayed from
              side to side in sorrow
trumpeting in forlorn baby voice
              his loss and deep distress.

The herd now approached
              His aunts folding him
lovingly in their trunks.
              We will be your mothers now.

Why, oh why my aunts
              why did they kill her
oh so brutally?
              And why did they cut
out her ivory tusks?

Oh little baby son
              Some humans have
Lost all feelings of love.

They want the ivory tusks
              to make trinkets and bangles
to adorn themselves
              and greedily gather money.

Sadly, the baby elephant said
               but aunts, they can fashion
Trinkets and bangles
               from crystal, gold and silver.

Why do they want to kill us
               just for our tusks?
What would they say and do
               if we cut out their teeth
to hang as a necklace
               round our own necks?

Baby, baby we do not
               know the answer.
We can only hope and pray
               that they find a way
back to understanding that
               every being, animal or human
has the right to live in
               peace and harmony together.

The herd moved on
               the baby tenderly protected
in their loving midst.

Will human beings heed
               this heartbreaking story?
Will they learn from these
               gentle intelligent giants?

Will they realise that
               we were meant to respect
all creatures of this planet
               and live in peace and harmony
with all of living beings?
               Will they,..................will they?

Life's Journey

The river of life
        serene and turbulent
flows through banks
        covered with rich
tapestries of years.

Proud swans glide by
        dressed in pristine white
bear the pictures
        of your journey.

Joyous laughter, vale of tears
        leisure, toil and duty
rewarded by honour and esteem.

Your advancing soul
        ever yearning for the stars
is helped on its voyage
        by mystic angels
draped in heavenly blue.

Teaching life's lessons
        to acquire knowledge
discover wisdom
        and find tolerance
compassion and love.

All this will lead
        your exalted soul
to the splendour and brilliance
        of everlasting life.

Ghosts of Yesteryear

A scent of pine
           of coffee, freshly ground
Was that a whiff of
           cigar I could smell?

The candles glowed
           their flickering flames
dancing golden sprites.

The ghost of Christmas past
           filed silently into the room
and hovered there
           bidding me to remember.

The music we played
           float through my mind
the sounds of a flute
           tambourines and bells.

Much laughter abounded
           if we sang out of tune
when we could not find
           the notes to Scarborough Fair.

Softly, barley perceived
    I hear the gypsy rover
come over the hill
    played on your recorder.

Carols of Christmas Angels
    resounded, full of joy
As we ended our concert
    on tha,t day so long ago

Still I hear the music
    still I hear the laughter
when the ghosts of yesteryear
    join me in the warmth of Christmas.

Gypsy Song

Gypsy with the sad
        far away look in the depths
of your dark eyes
        searching the far horizon.

Gypsy Troubadour, the locks
        of your dark hair
stir softly in the breeze.
        Your slender body
trembles with emotion.

Zigeuner, tell me the story
        of your wandering life
in the gaily painted wagons
        under the sun and the moon.

Tell me of the years
        of endless persecution.
Of the hounding and the hiding,
        of the pain and of the tears.

Zsygane, your melodious violin
        sings the haunting songs
of your silent dreams
        hidden in your heart.

Dreams of peace and joy
        of compassion and love.
Your violin sings your
        heartrending yearning
out into the universe.

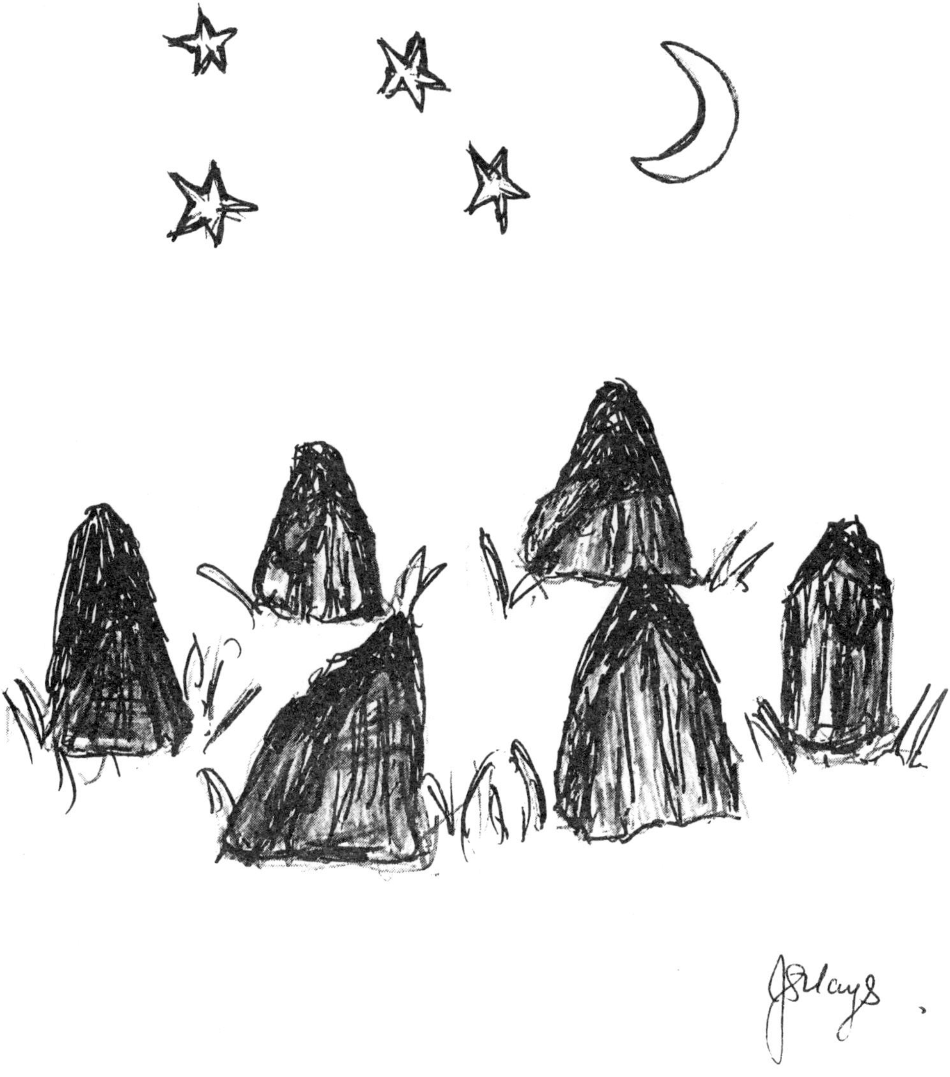

Midnight Prayer

The worshippers gathered
        in the ancient circle of stone
Their flowing white cloaks
        swirling in graceful folds.

Incandescent tongues of flame
        scattered across the fiery sky
as the burning globe of the sun
        sank slowly out of sight.

Fireflies skimmed through the air
        like a band of gleaming jewels
weaving and undulating
        through the ancient stones.

Darkness fell and lady Luna
        robed in luminescent silver
drew back the curtain of cloud
        and bade the stars enter.

Against the midnight velvet sky
        iridescent glowing stars
streamed forth in millions
        to join the Lady of Light.

While down below
        the candles had been lit
throwing tendrils of flame
        across the eerie stones.

Slowly the worshippers
           began to move
walking round and round
           the hallowed circle.

Their faces lifted to the sky
           melodious chanting
trembling in the air
           and rising on the ether.

Oh lovely Being of Light
           Clothed in glory
dressed in pristine white
           radiate your love and light
upon this dark dispirited earth.

Send down your angels
           to spread enlightenment
and waken peoples souls.

Suddenly the moon grew brighter
           darting lights shone, hovered
above the circles of stones.

The worshippers grew silent
           falling to their knees
in wonder and adoration.

A multitude of shooting stars
           left a trail of blazing fire
in a ring around the stones.

From the worshippers within
           a murmur rose in unison
thank God thank God
           our prayers have been answered.

Let us go forth now
            into the world
and spread our message
            of love and light.

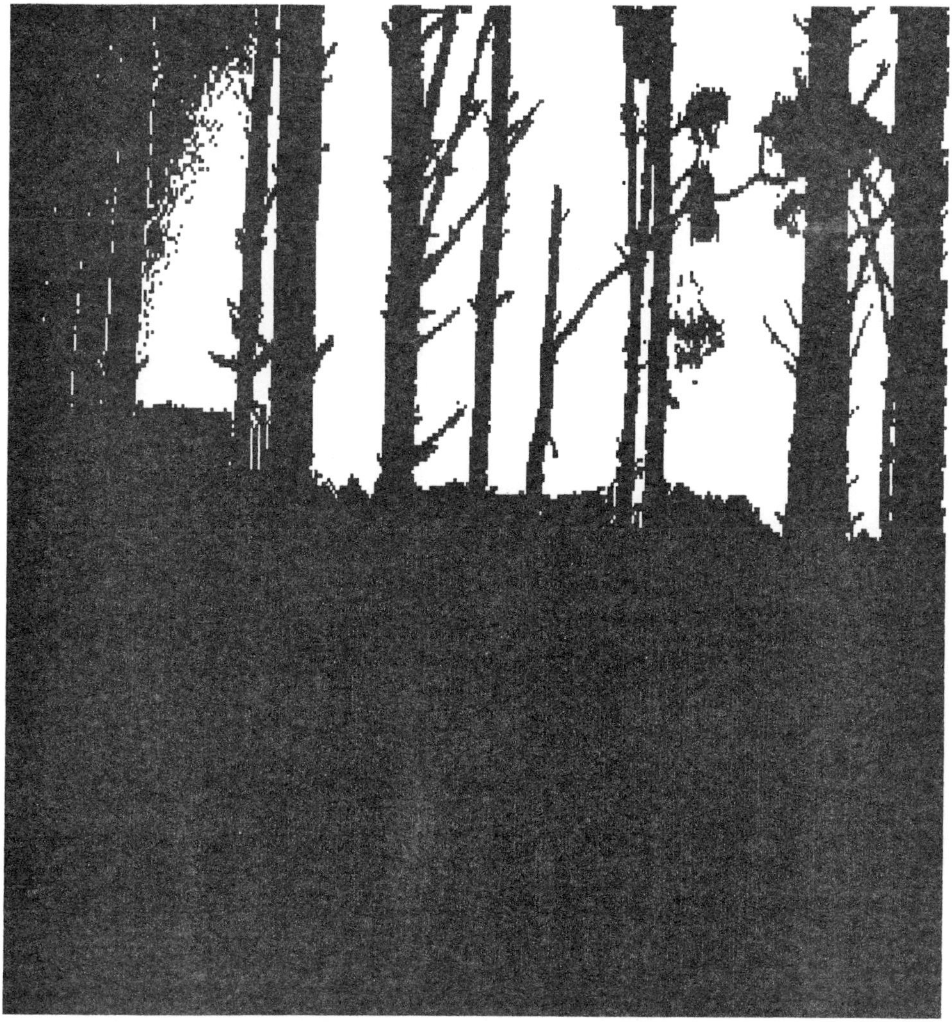

Enchanted Forest

Once we walked together
        in this enchanted forest
with arms entwined
        hearts filled with love.

Hand in hand we run
        like innocent children.
Laughing with joy
        as autumn leaves
swirled around our feet.

Our souls were one
        as we gazed and drowned
in the liquid pools
        of each others eyes.

We carved our names
        on our special tree
while the scent of pine and moss
        rose and perfumed the air.

Now I walk this path alone
        snow is falling in thick
star shaped flakes
        clothing the trees
in sparkling white garments.

I stand alone in this pristine
        crystal winter forest
and call your name...endlessly...
        my angel you took my heart
and left me standing
        waiting, grieving endlessly.....

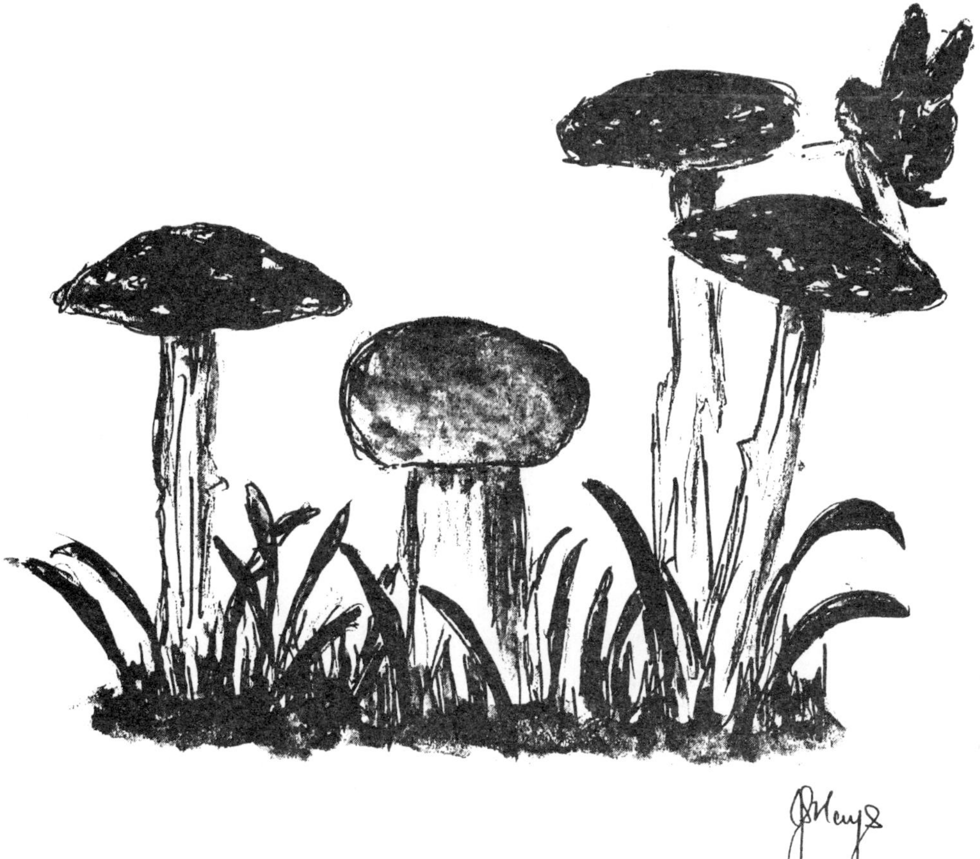

Summer Evening

The sun is going down
           Leaving trails of blazing fire
Red and pink across the sky.

Day is fading fast
           handing the heavens to the night
the mystery to unfold.

Dreamily, green fronds sway
           in the slowly flowing river
and weeping willows
           dip their branches in the water.

Stone angels guard
           the ancient church yard
township of departed souls.

Churchbells ring the hour,
           then all is quiet all is still.
Shadows deepen, darkness falls.

Then a golden shimmer
           lights the velvet sky
as the moon appears in all her glory.

Shining, palely glowing
           she lights the dark
and guards the secret of the night.

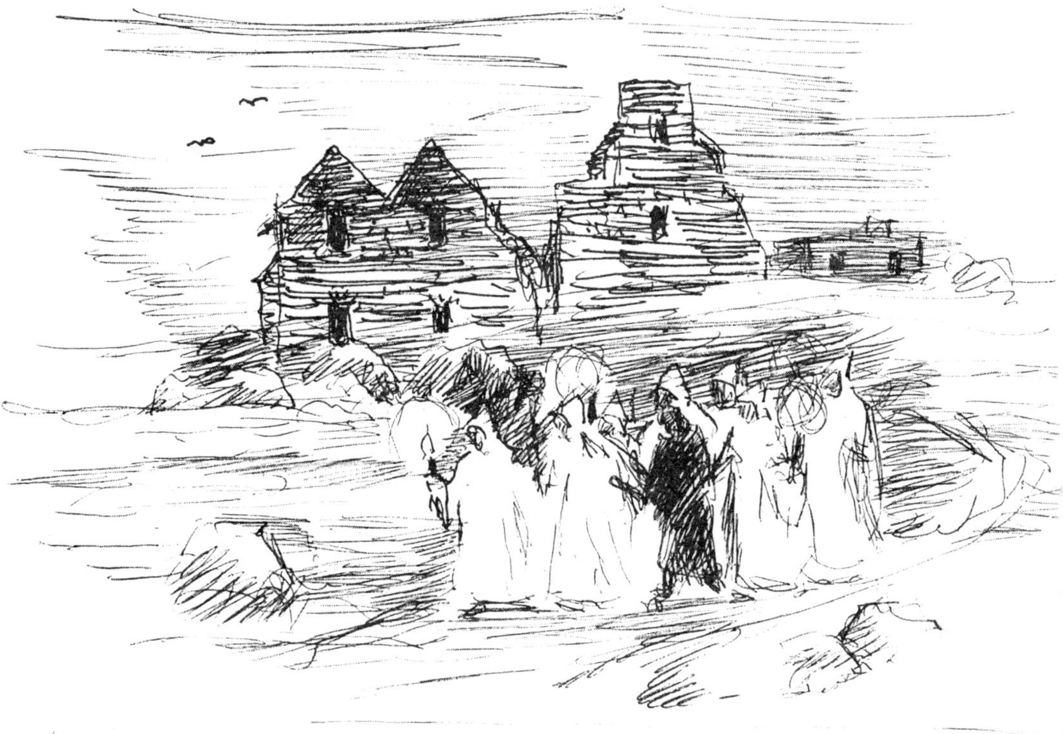

The Haunted Abbey

Dusk is spreading a shadowy cloak
        over the old abbey garden.
While wisps of white mist
        hover round the bushes
like spectres of another age.

The crumbling abbey walls
        rise darkly in the distance
empty now ... and silent.

Through the staring blackened windows
        which once were full of light
bats only now hold evensong.

And then ... like a whisper
        and an eerie sigh,
came the sound of chanting.

From the black abbey they came,
        monks in robes of white
holding flaming torches.

In cowled ghostly procession
        they float along the path
mythic unearthly phantoms.

One in their midst they dragged
        bare and shaven headed
clothed in rough dark rags.

You have sinned, they chanted.
        You must be punished
and darken our doors no more.

They thrust him out
              and turned about
in cowled ghostly procession.

Outside the walls
              the poor sinner on his knees
wails and begs forgiveness.

A shimmering Being
              takes his hands and
folds him in a mantle of love.

Come, he said those within
              should have forgiven you

the sinner lifts his eyes in awe
              to this Being of Light.
Please, he whispers forgive them too
              and end the nightly haunting.

From behind the drifting clouds
              The golden moon shone
through the branches of the trees.

The cowled ghostly procession
              filing past the abbey walls
repentant now... and silent,
              their eyes cast to the ground.

Suddenly, a beam of light
              fell on the penitent monks.
They stopped and lifted their heads
              in awe and disbelief,

and saw ... above them
        hands outstretched ...
the poor sinner they had
        thrust from their midst.

One by one he pulled them up
        in the beam of loving light
in unconditional compassion.

The shimmering Being
        drew angels wings
over the black haunted abbey.

All is forgiven now.
        All is love and peace.

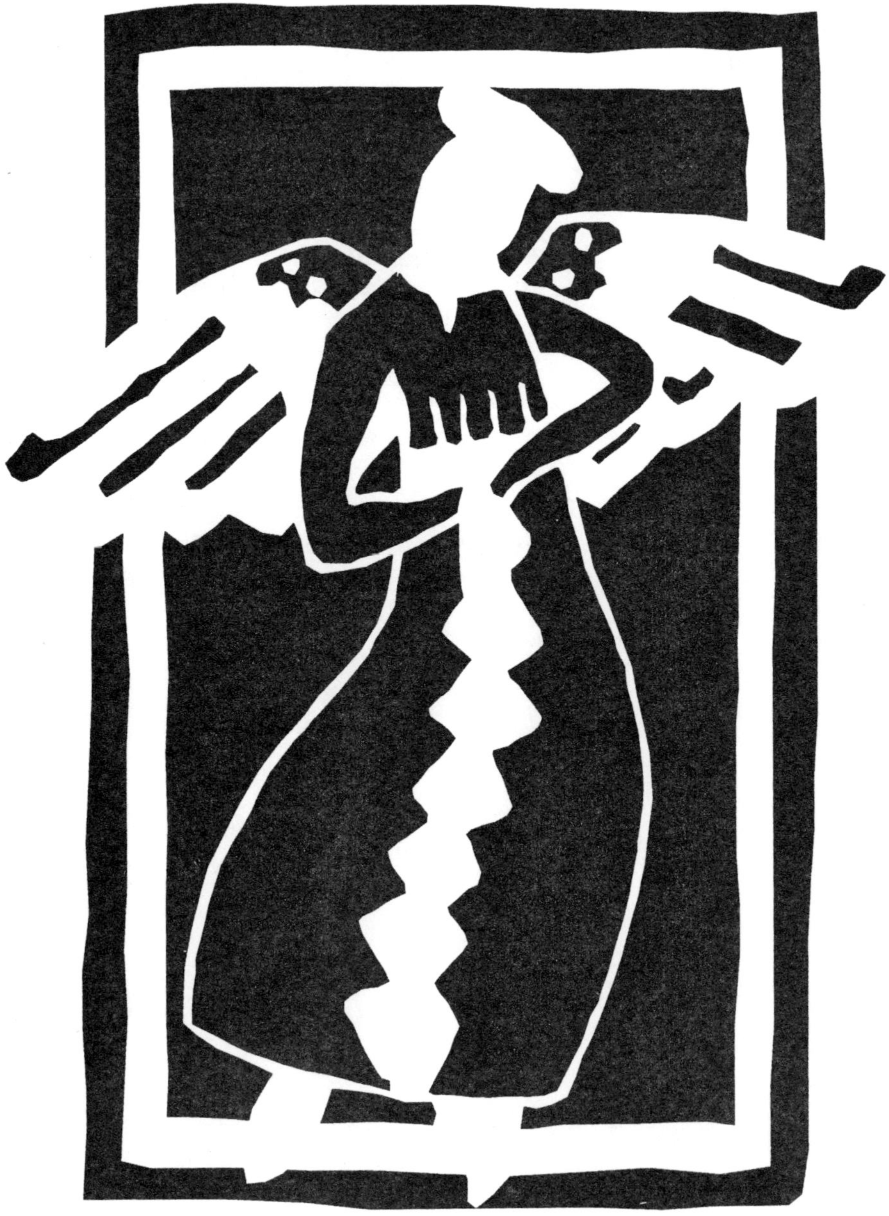

Angel Presence

Was that an angel
            hovering just there?

A glimpse, a breath, a touch
            of gossamer silk.

A swirl in the room
            a sudden flash of light.

A haunting sound
            of heavenly music.

Like a breathless whisper
            heard and then no more.

An outline, elfin, ethereal
            a tinkle of silver bells.

A rush of air and then
            I was alone again.

Earthbound Spirit

Angel of my dreams
        once you came to me
bound in the chains
        of your dark life.

Help me you cried,
        release me from the bondage
of my unhappiness.
        Heal my tormented heart.

Deep compassion filled my soul
        and I wrapped him in my love.
Come with me, I said
        I will take you to the light.

Let my spirit guide you
        let my love soothe your pain.
I will tell your story
        you have not lived in vain.

My dark angel wept and
        stretched out his trembling hands.
I took him in my arms
        and lifted him out of the night.

And he was folded in mystical wings
        he was bathed in golden light
as his spirit soared
        to other-worldly realms.

Leaving me gazing
        at the starlit sky
endlessly searching
        endlessly waiting
for the dark angel
        who came to me one night.

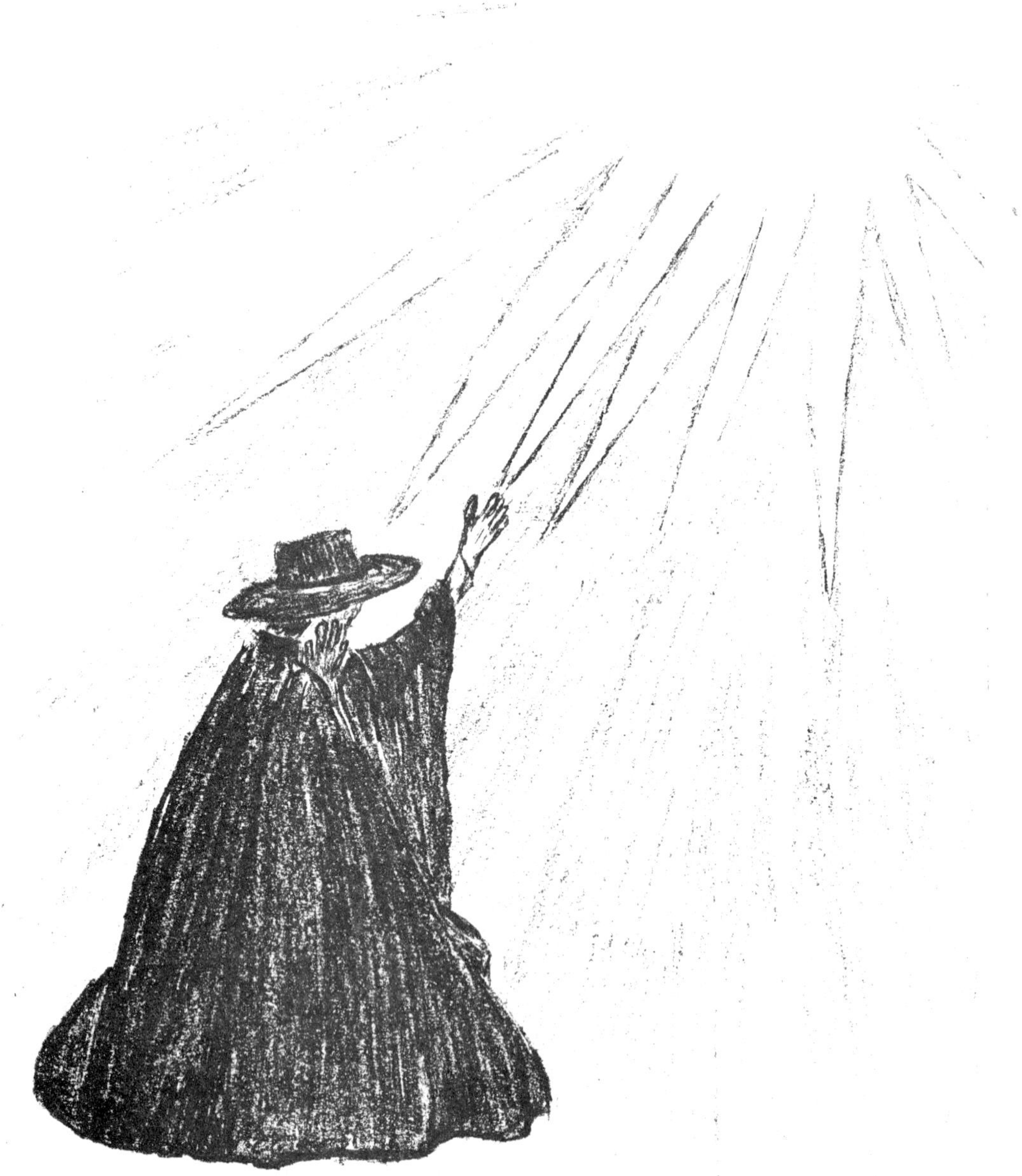

Spirit Rescue

Lured by haunting music
                so sweet but so sad
an angel descended from heaven.

He found a spirit weeping
                shrouded in robes of sorrow.
The angel sighed in deep compassion
                but could not help the spirit.

The help of a mortal was needed
                to lift this earthbound spirit
out of the darkness of despair.

The angel of light appeared
                at my open door
clasped in his wings
                he brought me the soul.

Help him he told me.
                Release him from his sorrow
and show him the way
                to the heavenly light.

I obeyed the angels request
                and freed the spirit from
the chains of desolation.

Joyful, with exultant eyes
                the spirit saw the angel.
Enfolded in his wings
                he spiralled and soared
to astral realms of light.

For Erik

T'is not the beauty of your face
          but the beauty of your soul
that shines in your eyes
          and illuminates your heart.

A beautiful face alone is
          nothing but the façade
which often hides
          an empty building.

But a soul full of love
          for all things divine
a soul full of music
          is a soul full of light.

We love you Erik for
          the beauty of your soul
your soul is immortal
          it has ascended to the light.

To shine down forever
          in limitless love
to unite all of us
          who love you now
and would have loved you then....

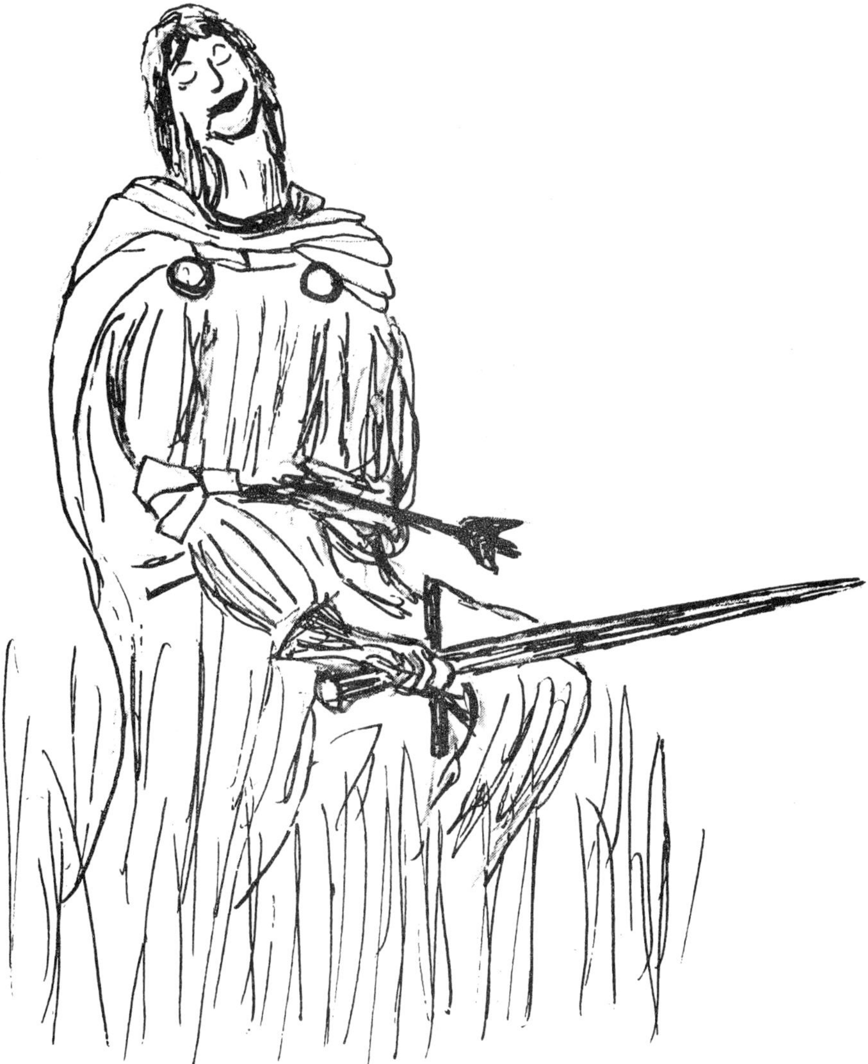

After The Battle

My lord, thou grievest my heart,
        For my honour didst thou fight
Upon this field of woe.

Upon this cursed field
        Where now thy body rests,
thy life's blood staining
        my favour, still entwined
Upon thy arm.

Oh, my Lord, what price honour.
        Now I am without thee.
Take me; let me die too,
        upon this cursed field.

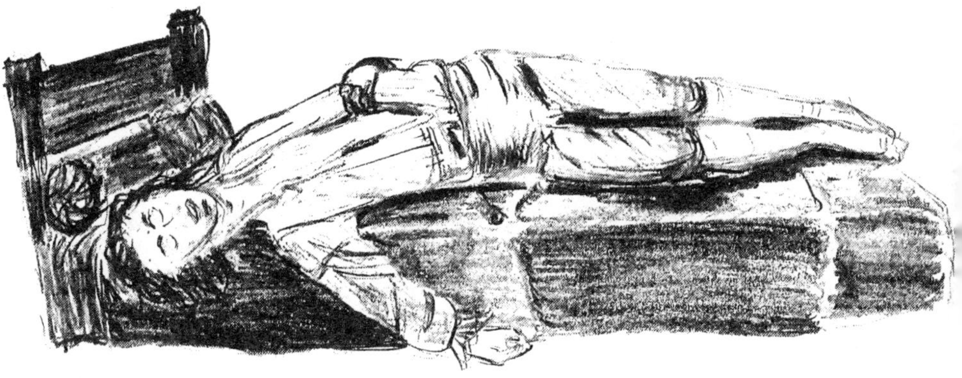

The Warrior's Return

The candles flicker and wave
        in this bare stone chamber.
Shadows deepen on the walls
        As I kneel before you.

They brought you after the battle
        and laid you upon this bench
your face as white as marble
        your hands so cold, so cold.

My beloved valiant knight
        I hold you in my tender arms
while the tears of my harrowed soul
        gleam upon your pallid face.

Oh, this howling torture
        this endless tormented grief
that encircles my heart
        in bands of cruel sorrow.

Why you my love, why you I cry
        Why you . . . and for what?
What have we won
        but an ocean of blood and tears.

I anoint your body in scented oils
        I clothe you in velvet and silk
And shower you with sweet blossoms . . .
        But wait...wait, where have you gone?

I know it looks like you
        and yet... you are not here.
This is but an empty shell
        where are you, oh, where are you?

Suddenly, in the candles feeble light
        a white mist hovers, trembling
undulating, writhing
        slowly taking shape.

A gossamer form emerges slowly
        can it be...can it be... is it you?
Then a whisper floats to me
        light as a breath of air.

My beloved lady, I am here
        yonder body in death's deep embrace
was but the temple of my soul.
        My spirit is with you forever.

Then the chamber bursts into light
        as a wondrous being enters,
robed in star studded veils
        radiating love, as yet unknown.

The chamber vibrates with his light
        and supernal angelic voices sing
as he gently folds my love, my knight
        inside his ethereal white wings.

Then an incandescent glow, a shining
        like a comet in the darkened sky
and then I am alone again
        kneeling by my lovers body.

Ah, but what joy, what rapture.
        He is not really dead,
but waiting for the day
        when my own immortal soul
joins him in our celestial home.

Loves's bondage

Once again, ensnared
           in the bonds of love.
These silken tendrils
           which promise bliss and joy.

Unsuspecting, the soul
           opens up to another
and the eternal dance begins.

All you see in the
           background of your mind
is the face of your inamorato.

Sleep bids a silent farewell
           as you whisper his name.
And all the food you need
           is love and music.

But beware! These silken threads
           oh so deceptively soft,
bind the heart in chains
           too strong to break.

Love, Amour,
           this fragile plant
which yet stirs passions tempests
           powerful fervent and fierce.

It is rapture, it's delight,
           It's warm affection
agony and anguish.
           It's grief and sorrow.

Love finds a way
           through the strongest armour
and ensnares your
           trusting unwary heart.

The Stranger

What is this feeling
          that encircles my heart
with strange fervent longing?

Why does a name
          that had no meaning
now sound so appealing.

Why does a face that
          was unknown before
suddenly become so precious?

Stealthy and unbidden, this
          feeling creeps into my heart
and hovers there
          like autumn mist.

The stranger I did
          not known before
is a stranger no more
          for the angel of love
has touched my soul
          and filled my heart
with delight.

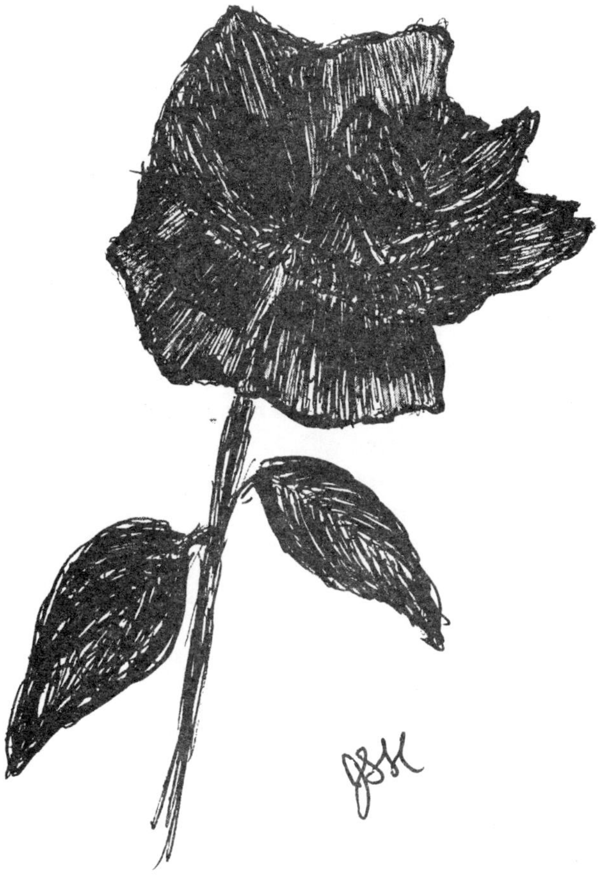

Lost Love

My old companion
        whose name I know so well
appears again before my eyes
        in the midnight darkness.

Cloaked and full of foreboding
        he stirs the dying embers
of the love
        that lost its way.

He shows me my unhappy heart
        which desperately tries
to hold together
        the shattered fragments
of a lovely dream.

He points to my
        sad and lonely soul,
to the wrenching pain
        and the howling grief.

He stands with me
        as, hollow eyed
bereft and forlorn
        I gaze at your receding form.

I cried . . . don't go, don't go
        my hands stretched out
to hold you back
        but all I had left to hold
were the ashes and embers
        of a love that lost its way.

His funereal presence
        is my constant companion
in the dark of the night
        and the light of day.

He leads me through vast caves
        black and cold as ice.
Through swirling mists
        and waterfalls of tears.

He holds my hand
        and his ghostly voice
whispers in my ear
        I am all you have left
to hold in this world.

The name of my cloaked friend?
        He is known as dark despair.
As his shadowed form
        surrounds me
he swings out his cloak
        to hide the love
that lost its way.

Eternal Love

You came to me
        like a whisper in the night,
from your other world
        and told me of your love.

Watch the petals of a rose
        unfolding in the sun
you will find my love
        in the sweet scent.

Watch the crystal waterfall
        sparkle and glisten
as it dances over the rocks.
        Open your heart and listen
to the music of my love.

Watch the wonder of the rainbow
        as it spans your world and mine.
See the glowing colours
        and read the message of my heart.

With the swirling mists
        I will embrace you.
With the jewelled stars
        I will light your way.

Like the night
        I will surround you
in a velvet cloak of love
        and for all eternity
I will protect you.

Then, when the angel of light
              wraps you in his silver wings
and brings you back to me
              I will take your hand in mine.

Together at last we will sing
              the symphony of our love.
Like a blazing comet it will fly
              across the mystic universe.

There forever to shine in glory
              to bear witness to our story
how the power of true love
              transcends beyond all reason
the boundaries of earth and heaven.

Night Magic

Love for you was born
                in my heart
like a sunburst
                like the petals
of a rose unfolding.

Like the stars
                flashing silver light
and the all knowing moon
                shrouded in the mists of night.

The night! The night
                is my friend.
For only in its velvet dark can
                the wings of my dreams
unfold, unfurl and find you.

Only in the vast halls
                Of darkness can
The flame of my love
                illuminate your heart.

Music of the night
                enfolds us in mystic fire
as, entranced, enslaved
                to its seductive sound
we dance and we sway
                in some enchanted
shimmering crystal haze.

And the all knowing moon
                and the stars
flashing silver light
                keep our secret
of the magic of the night.

The Long Search

I searched the midnight sky
                and asked the golden stars
to tell me where to find you.

I asked the lady of light
                enrobed in virgin white
where, oh where can I find you?

No answer came
                I stood alone in the dark
consumed with longing
                drowned in despair.

Then I asked the angels
                please help me to identify
the unique soul which is yours
                in propria persona.

Will I find you in the forest
                or on a busy street?
Was it the shape
                coming out of the shadow
or the figure that
                disappeared in the mist?

Would I see you
                at a gala performance
or in a crowded train?

I know when I find you
                trumpets will sound
and lightening strike
                my joyful soul.

Then, one fateful day
                I stood at the door
of a small dark room
                and heard a beautiful voice.

My soul flew to heaven
                I knew it was you.
But no lightening struck
                nor trumpets sound.

Unobtrusive and silent
                like a spectre of the night
love crept on velvet feet
                into my unsuspecting heart.

Now, wherever I am
                all I see is your face
and in the mirror of your eyes
                the beauty of your soul.

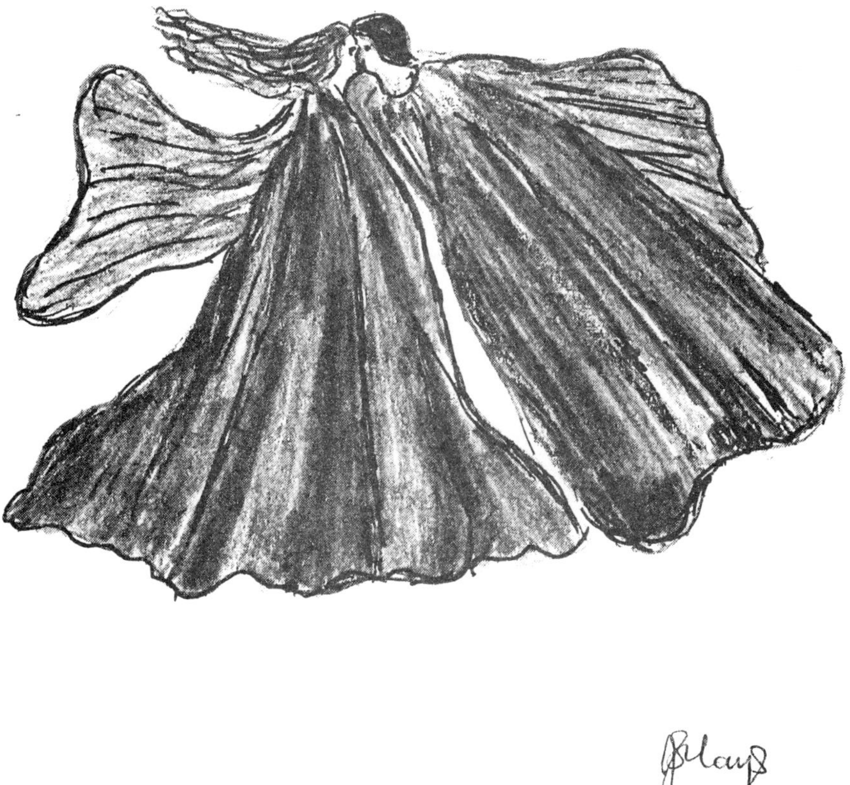

Stay with me

Spirit of my soul mate
           stay with me.

When the dark nights unfold,
           stay with me.

When storm clouds gather
           and lightening strikes
stay with me.

When thunder rips the sky apart
           stay with me.

Through the dance of life
           stay with me.

And when the reaper folds me
           in his dark embrace,
come for me.

And through the mists of eternity
           stay with me.

Half forgotten memory

As I sat dreaming
        here one night
by the candles flickering glow,
           curling tendrils of incense
drifting through the light.

I thought I heard my name
        like a long whispering sigh
trembling through the smoke
        remember me...remember me...

A half forgotten memory
        a fugitive shadow, hovering
clinging to my subconscious mind
        like strands of silken cobwebs.

Music from another realm
        trailing through my dreams.
Stirring an echo in my soul
        of a long forgotten love.

A face takes shape, then
        dissolves into nothing
leaving me feeling bereft
        yearning for I know no what.

Who is this spectre of the past
        that calls my name?
From the swirling mists of time
        who is this shade
who haunts my dreams
        like a half forgotten memory?
Remember me .... remember me...

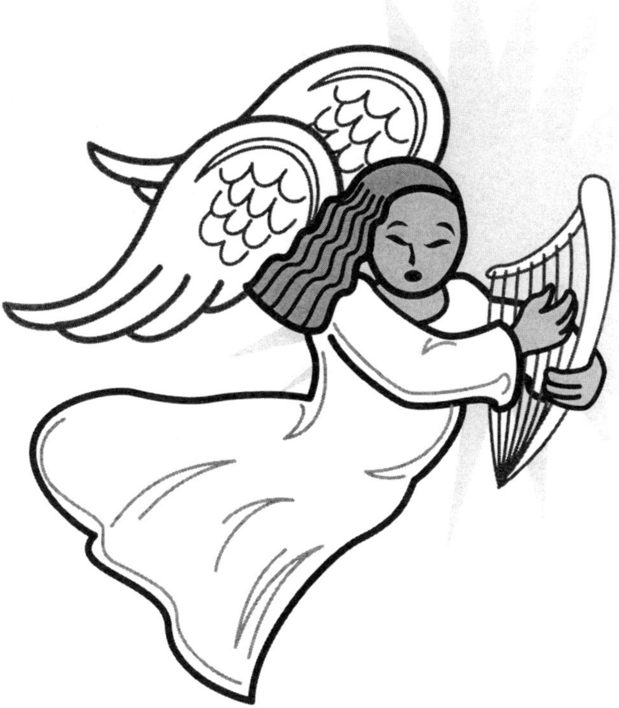